by Iain Gray

Lang**Syne**

PUBLISHING

WRITING *to* REMEMBER

Lang**Syne**

PUBLISHING

WRITING *to* REMEMBER

Vineyard Business Centre,
Pathhead, Midlothian EH37 5XP
Tel: 01875 321 203 Fax: 01875 321 233
E-mail: info@lang-syne.co.uk
www.langsyneshop.co.uk

Design by Dorothy Meikle
Printed by Montgomery Litho, Glasgow
© Lang Syne Publishers Ltd 2011

ISBN 978-1-85217-259-6

Kane

MOTTO:
A stroked cat is gentle.

CREST:
A mountain cat.

NAME variations include:
Ó Catháin *(Gaelic)*
Cahan
O'Cahan
O'Cain
McCain
Kayne
Keane

Chapter one:
Origins of Irish surnames

According to an old saying, there are two types of Irish – those who actually are Irish and those who wish they were.

This sentiment is only one example of the allure that the high romance and drama of the proud nation's history holds for thousands of people scattered across the world today.

It's a sad fact, however, that the vast majority of Irish surnames are found far beyond Irish shores, rather than on the Emerald Isle itself.

The population stood at around eight million souls in 1841, but today it stands at fewer than six million.

This is mainly a tragic consequence of the potato famine, also known as the Great Hunger, which devastated Ireland between 1845 and 1849.

The Irish peasantry had become almost wholly reliant for basic sustenance on the potato, first introduced from the Americas in the seventeenth century.

When the crop was hit by a blight, at least 800,000 people starved to death while an estimated two million others were forced to seek a new life far from their native shores – particularly in America, Canada, and Australia.

The effects of the potato blight continued until about 1851, by which time a firm pattern of emigration had become established.

Ireland's loss, however, was to the gain of the countries in which the immigrants settled, contributing enormously, as their descendants do today, to the well being of the nations in which their forefathers settled.

But those who were forced through dire circumstance to establish a new life in foreign parts never forgot their roots, or the proud heritage and traditions of the land that gave them birth.

Nor do their descendants.

It is a heritage that is inextricably bound up in the colourful variety of Irish names themselves – and the origin and history of these names forms an integral part of the vibrant drama that is the nation's history, one of both glorious fortune and tragic misfortune.

This history is well documented, and one of the most important and fascinating of the earliest sources are *The Annals of the Four Masters*, compiled between 1632 and 1636 by four friars at the Franciscan Monastery in County Donegal.

Compiled from earlier sources, and purporting to go back to the Biblical Deluge, much of the material takes in the mythological origins and history of Ireland and the Irish.

This includes tales of successive waves of invaders and settlers such as the Fomorians, the Partholonians, the Nemedians, the Fir Bolgs, the Tuatha De Danann, and the Laigain.

Of particular interest are the *Milesian Genealogies*,

because the majority of Irish clans today claim a descent from either Heremon, Ir, or Heber – three of the sons of Milesius, a king of what is now modern day Spain.

These sons invaded Ireland in the second millennium B.C, apparently in fulfilment of a mysterious prophecy received by their father.

This Milesian lineage is said to have ruled Ireland for nearly 3,000 years, until the island came under the sway of England's King Henry II in 1171 following what is known as the Cambro-Norman invasion.

This is an important date not only in Irish history in general, but for the effect the invasion subsequently had for Irish surnames.

'Cambro' comes from the Welsh, and 'Cambro-Norman' describes those Welsh knights of Norman origin who invaded Ireland.

But they were invaders who stayed, inter-marrying with the native Irish population and founding their own proud dynasties that bore Cambro-Norman names such as Archer, Barbour, Brannagh, Fitzgerald, Fitzgibbon, Fleming, Joyce, Plunkett, and Walsh – to name only a few.

These 'Cambro-Norman' surnames that still flourish throughout the world today form one of the three main categories in which Irish names can be placed – those of Gaelic-Irish, Cambro-Norman, and Anglo-Irish.

Previous to the Cambro-Norman invasion of the twelfth century, and throughout the earlier invasions and settlement of those wild bands of sea rovers known as the Vikings in the eighth and ninth centuries, the population of the island was relatively small, and it was normal for a person to be identified through the use of only a forename.

But as population gradually increased and there were many more people with the same forename, surnames were adopted to distinguish one person, or one community, from another.

Individuals identified themselves with their own particular tribe, or 'tuath', and this tribe – that also became known as a clann, or clan – took its name from some distinguished ancestor who had founded the clan.

The Gaelic-Irish form of the name Kelly, for example, is Ó Ceallaigh, or O'Kelly, indicating descent from an original 'Ceallaigh', with the 'O' denoting 'grandson of.' The name was later anglicised to Kelly.

The prefix 'Mac' or 'Mc', meanwhile, as with the clans of the Scottish Highlands, denotes 'son of.'

Although the Irish clans had much in common with their Scottish counterparts, one important difference lies in what are known as 'septs', or branches, of the clan.

Septs of Scottish clans were groups who often bore an entirely different name from the clan name but were under the clan's protection.

In Ireland, septs were groups that shared the same name and who could be found scattered throughout the four provinces of Ulster, Leinster, Munster, and Connacht.

The 'golden age' of the Gaelic-Irish clans, infused as their veins were with the blood of Celts, pre-dates the Viking invasions of the eighth and ninth centuries and the Norman invasion of the twelfth century, and the sacred heart of the country was the Hill of Tara, near the River Boyne, in County Meath.

Known in Gaelic as 'Teamhar na Rí', or Hill of Kings, it was the royal seat of the 'Ard Rí Éireann', or High King of Ireland, to whom the petty kings, or chieftains, from the island's provinces were ultimately subordinate.

It was on the Hill of Tara, beside a stone pillar known as the Irish 'Lia Fáil', or Stone of Destiny, that the High Kings were inaugurated and, according to legend, this stone would emit a piercing screech that could be heard all over Ireland when touched by the hand of the rightful king.

The Hill of Tara is today one of the island's main tourist attractions.

Opposition to English rule over Ireland, established in the wake of the Cambro-Norman invasion, broke out frequently and the harsh solution adopted by the powerful forces of the Crown was to forcibly evict the native Irish from their lands.

These lands were then granted to Protestant colonists, or 'planters', from Britain.

Many of these colonists, ironically, came from Scotland and were the descendants of the original 'Scotti', or 'Scots', who gave their name to Scotland after migrating there in the fifth century A.D., from the north of Ireland.

Colonisation entailed harsh penal laws being imposed on the majority of the native Irish population, stripping them practically of all of their rights.

The Crown's main bastion in Ireland was Dublin and its environs, known as the Pale, and it was the dispossessed peasantry who lived outside this Pale, desperately striving to eke out a meagre living.

It was this that gave rise to the modern-day expression of someone or something being 'beyond the pale'.

Attempts were made to stamp out all aspects of the ancient Gaelic-Irish culture, to the extent that even to bear a Gaelic-Irish name was to invite discrimination.

This is why many Gaelic-Irish names were anglicised with, for example, and noted above, Ó Ceallaigh, or O'Kelly, being anglicised to Kelly.

Succeeding centuries have seen strong revivals of Gaelic-Irish consciousness, however, and this has led to many families reverting back to the original form of their name, while the language itself is frequently found on the fluent tongues of an estimated 90,000 to 145,000 of the island's population.

Ireland's turbulent history of religious and political strife is one that lasted well into the twentieth century, a landmark century that saw the partition of the island into the twenty-six counties of the independent Republic of

Ireland, or Eire, and the six counties of Northern Ireland, or Ulster.

Dublin, originally founded by Vikings, is now a vibrant and truly cosmopolitan city while the proud city of Belfast is one of the jewels in the crown of Ulster.

It was Saint Patrick who first brought the light of Christianity to Ireland in the fifth century A.D.

Interpretations of this Christian message have varied over the centuries, often leading to bitter sectarian conflict – but the many intricately sculpted Celtic Crosses found all over the island are symbolic of a unity that crosses the sectarian divide.

It is an image that fuses the 'old gods' of the Celts with Christianity.

All the signs from the early years of this new millennium indicate that sectarian strife may soon become a thing of the past – with the Irish and their many kinsfolk across the world, be they Protestant or Catholic, finding common purpose in the rich tapestry of their shared heritage.

Chapter two:

Princes of Ulster

**The Gaelic form of the Kane name is Ó Catháin,
thought to stem from a word signifying 'battle' – an apt
designation for this great clan that for centuries held
sway in the northwest of the province of Ulster in the
area of present day County Londonderry, or Derry.**

A separate sept of the clan, distinguished today by the
spelling 'Keane', or 'O'Keane', also flourished further
south in the provinces of Connacht and Munster.

The roots of the sept that would become known as
Princes of Ulster are truly aristocratic, with a descent from
the celebrated Niall Noíghiallach, better known to posterity
as the great warrior king Niall of the Nine Hostages, through
Eogan, one of his twelve sons.

The dramatic life and times of this ancestor of the Kanes
are steeped in stirring Celtic myth and legend.

The youngest son of Eochaidh Mugmedon, king of the
province of Connacht, his mother died in childbirth and he was
brought up by his evil stepmother Mongfhinn who, for reasons
best known to herself, was determined that he should die.

She accordingly abandoned him naked on the Hill of
Tara, inauguration site of the Ard Rí, or High Kings, of
Ireland, but he was was found by a wandering bard and
taken back to his father.

One legend is that Mongfhinn sent Niall and his four brothers – Brian, Fiachra, Ailill, and Fergus – to a renowned prophet who was also a blacksmith to determine which of them would succeed their father as Ard Rí.

The blacksmith, known as Sitchin, set the lads a task by deliberately setting fire to his forge.

Niall's brothers ran in and came out carrying the spearheads, fuel, hammers, and barrels of beer that they had rescued, but Niall staggered out clutching the heavy anvil so vital to the blacksmith's trade.

By this deed, Sitchin prophesied that Niall would be the one who would take on the glorious mantle of kingship.

Another prophetic incident occurred one day while Niall and his brothers were engaged in the hunt.

Thirsty from their efforts they encountered an ugly old woman who offered them water – but only in return for a kiss.

Three of the lads, no doubt repelled by her green teeth and scaly skin, refused; Fiachra pecked her lightly on the cheek and, by this act, she prophesied that he would one day reign at Tara – but only briefly.

The bold Niall, however, kissed her fully on the lips.

The hag then demanded that he should now have full sexual intercourse with her and, undaunted, he did so.

Through this action she was suddenly transformed into a stunningly beautiful young woman known as Flaithius, or Royalty, who predicted that he would become the greatest High King of Ireland.

His stepmother Mongfhinn later tried to poison him, but accidentally took the deadly potion herself and died.

This legend relates to what was known as the Festival of Mongfhinn, or Feis na Samhan (the Fest of Samhain), because it was on the evening of October 31, on Samhain's Eve, that the poisoning incident is said to have taken place.

It was believed for centuries in Ireland that, on Samhain Eve, Mongfhinn's warped and wicked spirit would roam the land in hungry search of children's souls.

The Festival, or Feast, of Samhain, is today better known as Halloween.

Niall became Ard Rí in 379 A.D. and embarked on the series of military campaigns and other daring adventures that would subsequently earn him the title of Niall of the Nine Hostages.

The nine countries and territories into which he raided and took hostages for ransom were the Irish provinces of Munster, Leinster, Connacht, and Ulster, Britain, and the territories of the Saxons, Morini, Picts, and Dalriads.

Niall's most famous hostage was a young lad known as Succat, son of Calpernius, a Romano-Briton who lived in the area of present day Milford Haven, on the Welsh coast.

Later known as Patricius, or Patrick, he became renowned as Ireland's patron saint, St. Patrick, responsible for bringing the light of Christianity to the island in the early years of the fifth century A.D.

Raiding in Gaul, in the area of Boulogne-sur-mer in

present day France, Niall was ambushed and killed by one of his treacherous subjects in 405 A.D.

From Niall's son Eogan came Cathain, who gave his name to the clan; He, in turn, was a descendant of Fergal mac Mael Duin, the Ard Rí, or High King of Ireland, who died in about 772 A.D. and who was ancestor of the powerful and illustrious dynasty known as the Uí Néill, or the O'Neills.

It was through this connection with the O'Neills that the Kanes held the hereditary and highly honoured post of officiating at the inauguration ceremonies of the O'Neill kings.

The ceremony involved the curious rite of the Kane chieftain throwing a shoe over the O'Neill chieftain's head in recognition of his sovereignty.

Serving as sub-kings under the O'Neills, the territory of the Kanes, centred on Limavady, became known as Ó Catháin's Country, and the sept ruled as virtual princes.

The ancient presence of these Princes of Ulster – of whom the proud MacCloskeys and MacAvinnys are branches – is recalled in both legend and the very landscape itself.

Dungiven Priory is reputed to contain the tomb of Cooey-na-Gal O'Cahan, who died circa 1385; an indication of his fearsome reputation is that 'Cooey-na-Gal' translates as 'Terror of the Stranger.'

'Limavady' itself is said to stem from the stirring tale of

how a Kane chieftain was rescued from near certain death at the hands of ambushers after his Irish wolfhound made a spectacular leap across a gorge on the River Roe.

The hound was able to alert its master's kinsfolk to their chieftain's plight.

Yet another legend relates to the hauntingly beautiful ballad *Finvola, The Gem of the Roe*, composed by the celebrated Kane harpist Toal Ó Catháin.

Finvola was the daughter of a Kane chieftain and, when she married one of the MacDonald Lords of Islay, off the western seaboard of Scotland, it was agreed that when she died and in keeping with family custom, her body would be returned for burial in her native land.

Several years passed until one evening the dread sound of the Kane banshee, or spirit, was heard crying mournfully; the banshee was only heard when a Kane had died, and it was quickly ascertained its cries could only pertain to the beautiful Finvola.

Crossing to Islay a party of Kanes found that Finvola had indeed died; her grief stricken husband had been unable to part with her body but following the impassioned pleas of her kin he agreed for her to be returned for burial in her native soil.

The Kane motto is 'A stroked cat is gentle', and its crest is a mountain cat – but also found on the family Coat of Arms is a curious symbol known as the Red Hand of Ulster.

There are several theories as to the origin and meaning

of the upraised right hand, palm facing outwards, but the one held by Kane genealogical researchers to be the most likely is a Biblical one that relates to Psalm 98:1:

> *O Sing unto the Lord a new song:*
> *For he hath done marvellous things*
> *His right hand and his holy arm,*
> *Hath gotten him the victory.*

Chapter three:

The last lament

**What has proven to have sown the seeds of the eventual
downfall of proud native Irish clans such as the Kanes
came in the wake of the Cambro-Norman invasion of
the late twelfth century, and the consolidation of the
power of the English Crown over the island.**

Twelfth century Ireland was far from being a unified
nation, split up as it was into territories ruled over by
squabbling chieftains such as Dermot MacMurrough, who
ruled as kings in their own right – and this inter-clan rivalry
worked to the advantage of the invaders.

In a series of bloody conflicts one chieftain, or king,
would occasionally gain the upper hand over his rivals,
and by 1156 the most powerful was Muirchertach
MacLochlainn, king of the powerful O'Neills.

The equally powerful Rory O'Connor, king of the
province of Connacht, opposed him but he increased his
power and influence by allying himself with Dermot
MacMurrough, king of Leinster.

MacLochlainn and MacMurrough were aware that the
main key to the kingdom of Ireland was the thriving trading
port of Dublin that had been established by invading
Vikings, or Ostmen, in 852 A.D.

Dublin was taken by the combined forces of the Leinster

and Connacht kings, but when MacLochlainn died the Dubliners rose up in revolt and overthrew MacMurrough.

A triumphant Rory O'Connor entered Dublin and was later inaugurated as Ard Rí, but the proud Dermott MacMurrough was not one to humbly accept defeat.

It was now that he appealed for help from England's Henry II in unseating O'Connor, an act that was to radically affect the future course of Ireland's fortunes.

The English monarch agreed to help MacMurrough, but distanced himself from direct action by delegating his Norman subjects in Wales with the task.

These ambitious and battle-hardened barons and knights had first settled in Wales following the Norman Conquest of England in 1066 and, with an eye on rich booty, plunder, and lands, were only too eager to obey their sovereign's wishes and furnish aid to MacMurrough.

MacMurrough crossed the Irish Sea to Bristol, where he rallied powerful barons such as Robert Fitzstephen and Maurice Fitzgerald to his cause, along with Gilbert de Clare, Earl of Pembroke.

The mighty Norman war machine soon moved into action, and so fierce and disciplined was their onslaught on the forces of Rory O'Connor and his allies that by 1171 they had re-captured Dublin, in the name of MacMurrough, and other strategically important territories.

It was now that a nervous Henry II began to take cold feet over the venture, realising that he may have created a rival in the form of a separate Norman kingdom in Ireland.

Accordingly, he landed on the island, near Waterford, at the head of a large army in October of 1171 with the aim of curbing the power of his Cambro-Norman barons.

Protracted war between the king and his barons was averted, however, when the barons submitted to the royal will, promising homage and allegiance in return for holding the territories they had conquered in the king's name.

Henry also received the submission and homage of many of the Irish chieftains, while English dominion over Ireland was ratified through the Treaty of Windsor of 1175, under the terms of which Rory O'Connor, for example, was allowed to rule territory unoccupied by the Normans in the role of a vassal of the king.

All that had been created was a simmering cauldron of discontent – one that would boil over periodically in subsequent centuries with particularly dire consequences for the Kanes and other Irish clans.

For centuries after the Norman invasions and the consolidation of power of the English Crown, native Irish chieftains had to walk a tightrope in attempting to retain their ancient rights and privileges.

This often meant seeking accommodation with the Crown by paying lip-service loyalty that would be rewarded with honours and titles – but what eventually shattered this tenuous bond was the odious scheme known as 'plantation.'

This policy of settling, or 'planting' loyal Protestants on Irish soil – on land that had been owned for centuries by the native families – had started during the reign from 1491 to 1547 of Henry VIII, whose Reformation effectively outlawed the established Roman Catholic faith throughout his dominions.

This settlement of Protestants in Ireland continued throughout the subsequent reigns of Elizabeth I, James I (James VI of Scotland), and Charles 1.

It was a policy that had truly devastating consequences for the Kanes of Ulster.

A number of Irish earls, supported by Donnell Ballagh Ó Catháin, rebelled against the policy of plantation but, following their defeat at the battle of Kinsale in 1601 and the final suppression of the rebellion three years later in Ulster, their future existence hung by a precarious thread.

Three years later, in September of 1607 and in what is known as The Flight of the Earls, Hugh O'Neill, 2nd Earl of Tyrone and Rory O'Donnell, 1st Earl of Tyrconnel, sailed into foreign exile from the village of Rathmullan, on the shore of Lough Swilly, in Co. Donegal.

Donnell Ballagh Ó Catháin had been forced into reluctant surrender during the abortive rebellion.

Despite the added indignity of also having to surrender much of his lands to the Crown, he was later incarcerated in the grim confines of the Tower of London, where he died, a broken man, in 1617.

He was the last of the Kane chieftains, and his part in the abortive rebellion only served to help accelerate the policy of plantation in Ulster under James I.

In a further insurrection that exploded in 1641, at least 2,000 Protestant settlers were massacred at the hands of Catholic landowners and their native Irish peasantry, while thousands more were driven from their lands to seek refuge where they could.

Terrible as the atrocities were against the Protestant settlers, subsequent accounts became greatly exaggerated, serving to fuel a burning desire on the part of Protestants for revenge against the rebels.

Tragically for Ireland, this revenge became directed not only against the rebels, but native Irish Catholics such as the Kanes in general.

The English Civil War intervened to prevent immediate action against the rebels, but following the execution of Charles I in 1649 and the consolidation of the power of England's fanatically Protestant Oliver Cromwell, the time was ripe for revenge.

The Lord Protector, as he was named, descended on Ireland at the head of a 20,000-strong army that landed at Ringford, near Dublin, in August of 1649.

He had three main aims: to quash all forms of rebellion, to 'remove' all Catholic landowners who had taken part in the rebellion, and to attempt to convert the native Irish to the Protestant faith.

This Cromwellian invasion was all too brutally successful, and it was the final nail in the coffin of the Kanes.

Their ancient homelands were lost forever, but their proud heritage was destined to live on through what is not only the last lament of the Kanes but also the Emerald Isle's most famous ballad.

This is none another than the haunting refrain of *Danny Boy*.

It is a ballad with a complex and curious genesis – the lyrics first being written in 1910 by an obscure English lawyer by the name of Frederic Edward Weatherley to a totally different tune to the one we know today.

The song proved unsuccessful commercially until a relative of Weatherley furnished him with the music of an old melody that is now known as the *Londonderry Air*.

Weatherley adapted his lyrics to fit the melody of the *Londonderry Air* and the result became the song now known today worldwide as *Danny Boy*.

But where did the tune known as the *Londonderry Air* originate?

The source is believed to have been a lament known as *O'Cahan's Lament*, composed by the Kane family bard Rory Dall O'Cahan, in the wake of the death of the last clan chieftain, Donnell Ballagh Ó Catháin, and the subsequent collapse of the fortunes of the proud and ancient family.

Chapter four:
On the world stage

Far from the tragedies of the past, bearers of the surname Kane have flourished in a wide range of pursuits, not least in the fields of acting, music, and sport.

The winner of an impressive two Emmy awards for her role as the wife of Latka Gravas on the popular American television comedy series *Taxi*, **Carol Kane** was born in 1952 in Cleveland, Ohio.

The actress also appeared in the Broadway musical *Wicked*, and was nominated for an Academy Award for her role in the 1975 movie *Hester Street*.

Born in 1973, **Bradley Caleb Kane** is the multi-talented writer, singer, and actor who provided the singing voice for *Aladdin* in the 1992 Disney animated feature of that name, while a year later he performed in the Broadway revival of *She Loves Me*.

Adelaide Kane, born in 1990, in Claremont, Western Australia, is the young actress whose first major role was playing the part of Lolly Allen in the immensely popular Australian television soap, *Neighbours*, while **Samuel Kane**, born in 1969, is the British actor who has appeared in a number of equally popular British television soaps, including *Coronation Street* and *Brookside*.

His wife is the former glamour model, and now television soap actress, Linda Lusardi.

Behind the lens, **Joseph Kane**, born in 1894 in San Diego and who died in 1975, was the American film editor, screenwriter, and director who, in addition to directing the 1935 *The Fighting Marines*, directed a number of Western movies.

Famous actors who worked under his direction included Roy Rogers, John Wayne, Gene Autry, and Walter Brennan.

In the world of popular music, **Helen Kane**, born Helen Schroeder in 1903 in the Bronx, New York to a German father and an Irish mother, was the singer best known for her hit *I Wanna Be Loved By You*.

It was her 'boop-boop-a-boop' singing style that made her the inspiration for the animated character Betty Boop in the 1928 musical *Good Boy*. She died in 1966.

Also in the world of animation and cartoons, **Bob Kane**, born Robert Kahn in 1915 and who died in 1998, was the American comic book artist and writer whose most famous creation – in collaboration with writer Bill Finger – was DC Comics' superhero *Batman*.

In contemporary times, Scottish brothers **Pat** and **Greg Kane**, born respectively in 1964 and 1966 near Glasgow, are the musicians who formed the highly successful pop group Hue and Cry.

The younger brother is a classically trained pianist, while Pat Kane has also pursued a career as a commentator on cultural and political issues.

Born in 1974 in Dallas, Texas, **Christian Kane** is not only the actor best known for his role as the lawyer Lindsey McDonald in the American television series *Angel*, but also as the lead singer of the rock band *Kane*, while **Arthur Kane**, born in the Bronx, New York, in 1949, was the bass guitarist for the American glam rock band The New York Dolls.

He died in 2004.

The Kanes also have a link to The Beatles – in the form of journalist and author **Larry Kane**, born in 1942, who was the only American reporter allowed to accompany the band on their famous North American tour of 1964.

He subsequently documented the experience in his best-selling book *Ticket to Ride*.

Another close observer of the music scene was **Art Kane**, born Arthur Kanofsky in New York City in 1925, and who died in 1995.

As a fashion and music photographer he took famous photographs of stars such as Bob Dylan, The Rolling Stones, and The Who.

Arguably his most famous work, however, is his photographic portrait of 57 jazz musicians in New York's Harlem district; published by Esquire magazine in 1958, it later formed the basis of the critically acclaimed film documentary *A Great Day in Harlem*.

Also in the world of creative art, **John Kane**, born in Scotland in 1860 and who immigrated to America when aged 19, is recognised today as having been an expert in the painting genre known as primitivism.

Born in Mallow, Co. Cork, in 1810, by the time of his death in 1871 **Paul Kane** would have become one of Canada's greatest painters.

It was some time between 1819 and 1822 when his parents emmigrated to Upper Canada from Ireland and settled in York – later to become the great city of Toronto.

His father earned a comfortable living as a wine and spirits merchant and was able to indulge his son's passion for art by helping to fund a study trip throughout Europe.

Returning to Canada, Kane travelled throughout the northwest in 1845 and from 1846 until 1848. Along the way he sketched the native inhabitants and their way of life, and these sketches later formed the basis of a vast collection of oil paintings.

From the world of art to the competitive world of sport, **Damien Kane**, born in 1960, is the American professional wrestler also known as 'The Godfather of Professional Wrestling', or 'The Godfather of Extreme', while **Dene O'Kane**, born in 1963, is the New Zealander who has reached the quarterfinals of the World Snooker Championship on two separate occasions.

In the boxing ring, **Justin Kane**, born in 1981 in Ferntree Gully, Victoria, is the Australian boxer who took the gold medal in the bantamweight division at the Commonwealth Games in 2002, while **Peter Kane**, born in

Heywood, Lancashire, was the English flyweight boxer who held he world championship title from 1938 to 1943.

On the golf course, **Lorie Kane**, born in 1964 in Charlottetown, Prince Edward Island, Canada, is the female professional golfer who was honoured with membership of the prestigious Order of Canada in 2006.

On the football pitch, **Tony Kane**, born in Belfast in 1987, is the Northern Irish full-back who, at the time of writing, plays for Blackburn Rovers, while **Tommy Kane**, born in Montreal in 1964, is the former American football player who played for five seasons with the Seattle Seahawks.

In the scientific laboratory, **Sir Robert Kane**, born in 1890, was a noted Irish chemist, while in contemporary times a leading light in the world of philosophy is American **Robert Kane**, born in 1938, and the author of a range of philosophical texts that include the 1985 *Free Will and Values* and the 1994 *Through the Moral Maze*.

Kane County in Utah is named after **Thomas L. Kane**, who was born in Philadelphia in 1822 and who died in 1883.

A lawyer, abolitionist, and army officer he was also instrumental in aiding the western migration in America of the Latter-day Saint movement.

A friend of the Mormon Church founder Brigham Young, the Thomas L. Kane Memorial Chapel in Kane, Pennsylvania is also named after him, while there is a statue to his honour as a 'friend of the Mormons' in Utah's Capitol Building.

His brother, **Elisha Kane**, born in 1820 and who died in 1850, served as a medical officer in the United States Navy, becoming Assistant Surgeon in the navy in 1843.

In addition to his involvement in the unsuccessful attempts to find the missing Arctic explorer Sir John Franklin, he also published the two-volume *Arctic Explorations*.

Also at sea, **Richard O'Kane**, born in 1911 in Dover, New Hampshire, and who died in 1994, was the Second World War United States Navy submarine commander who directly took part in more successful attacks on Japanese shipping than any other submarine officer.

No account of notable Kanes could perhaps be complete without reference to a film that has been placed by the American Film Institute at number one in its list of the 100 greatest American movies of all time.

The film, of course, is the 1941 mystery/drama **Citizen Kane**, released and directed by Orson Welles and with Welles in the lead role of fictional publishing magnate Charles Foster Kane.

The character is thought to have been modelled on a number of famous real life figures, including the newspaper magnate William Randolph Hearst and the aerospace and film industry tycoon Howard Hughes.

Key dates in Ireland's history from the first settlers to the formation of the Irish Republic:

circa 7000 B.C.	Arrival and settlement of Stone Age people.
circa 3000 B.C.	Arrival of settlers of New Stone Age period.
circa 600 B.C.	First arrival of the Celts.
200 A.D.	Establishment of Hill of Tara, Co. Meath, as seat of the High Kings.
circa 432 A.D.	Christian mission of St. Patrick.
800-920 A.D.	Invasion and subsequent settlement of Vikings.
1002 A.D.	Brian Boru recognised as High King.
1014	Brian Boru killed at battle of Clontarf.
1169-1170	Cambro-Norman invasion of the island.
1171	Henry II claims Ireland for the English Crown.
1366	Statutes of Kilkenny ban-marriage between native Irish and English.
1529-1536	England's Henry VIII embarks on religious Reformation.
1536	Earl of Kildare rebels against the Crown.
1541	Henry VIII declared King of Ireland.
1558	Accession to English throne of Elizabeth I.
1565	Battle of Affane.
1569-1573	First Desmond Rebellion.
1579-1583	Second Desmond Rebellion.
1594-1603	Nine Years War.
1606	Plantation' of Scottish and English settlers.